The Coping Skills Workbook

By Lisa M. Schab, LCSW

Childswork ™
ChildsPLAY

CALL 1·800·962·1141

A Brand of The Guidance Group

www.guidance-group.com

The Coping Skills Workbook
by Lisa M. Schab, LCSW

Childswork/Childsplay publishes products for mental health professionals, teachers, and parents who wish to help children with their developmental, social, and emotional growth. For questions, comments, or to request a free catalog describing hundreds of games, toys, books, and other counseling tools, call 1-800-962-1141.

© 1996 Childswork/Childsplay
A Brand of The Guidance Group
www.guidance-group.com

All rights reserved.
Printed in the United States of America

ISBN 10: 1-882732-56-1
ISBN 13: 978-1-882732-56-2

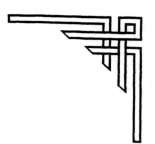

INTRODUCTION FOR ADULTS

The Coping Skills Workbook is designed to help instill in children the basic tools for emotional self-care.

In a world of crowded classrooms, working parents and split family units, children often become "street smart" without becoming "heart smart." They may know how to use a microwave and a video cassette recorder but they do not know how to calm themselves down when they are frustrated. They may know how to dial a pager number and to take a bus across town but they do not know how to deal with sadness and loss, disappointment and stress.

Children with a low frustration tolerance are at a greater risk for substance abuse because they are in greater need of an escape, a quick fix, something to help them cope.

Those children who are competent at nurturing themselves and caring for themselves on the "inside" and who feel confident in their ability to do so are less likely to turn to alcohol and drugs or develop eating disorders, depression or anxiety problems. Children who can identify and accept their feelings are more able to verbalize their needs and to have them met in an acceptable manner, instead of acting them out dangerously or disruptively.

The Coping Skills Workbook can be used as a method of intervention in helping the child who already exhibits coping problems. Ideally, it will be used with all children to prevent problems before they arise. It is intended to be used by a child with guidance from an adult.

Note: The objectives of all exercises in this book are to give children a chance to actively participate in their learning experience, thereby helping them to more fully understand the concepts put forth and to raise their self-esteem.

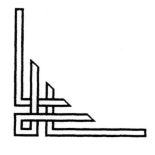

INTRODUCTION FOR KIDS

When we are very little, we don't know much about taking care of ourselves. For example, we don't know how to feed ourselves, or how to dress ourselves, or even how to brush our own teeth.

But as we grow up, we get smarter and stronger, and we learn to do these things. When we take care of our bodies in the right way, we are able to stay clean and healthy, comfortable and safe—on the outside.

It is also important to take care of ourselves on the inside. When we take care of our thoughts and feelings, we are able to stay peaceful and healthy, comfortable and safe—on the inside.

This is a book designed to help you learn different ways to take care of yourself on the inside. Taking care of your thoughts and feelings helps you to deal with problems. This is also known as "coping." In this book, you will learn about nine different coping skills, and then you will be given the chance to practice using them.

As you go through this book, there might be ideas that are new to you or that you don't understand right away. If that happens, you can ask an adult to explain them to you. Ask as many questions as you need to until you understand the idea. (Asking for help is one of the coping skills that this book teaches. It is one way to take care of yourself on the inside.)

Once you have learned these coping skills, you can practice them in any problem situation you encounter. The more you practice, the better you will get at using them, and the more confident you will feel in taking care of yourself. They are tools you will have for the rest of your life.

COPING SKILL 1:

DEAL WITH YOUR FEELINGS

Feelings are very important. When we pay attention to them, they can help us understand what we want or need. If you don't know what you need, then you won't know how to take care of yourself. If you know what you need, you can figure out the best way to get it.

There are four steps to dealing with your feelings:

1) Name them. Label what you are feeling.

2) Accept them. Remember that it's OK to feel this way.

3) Express them. Let your feelings out in a safe way.

4) Decide what you need to feel better. Use what you know about how you feel to tell you

what you need.

1. Name your feelings.

Objective: To help children differentiate between and learn the names of different feelings.

Can you tell which feeling is being expressed on these faces? Write your answers in the spaces below.

_____   _____   _____   _____   _____

HAPPY
SCARED
SAD MAD

Objective: To help children identify their own feelings and to learn new ones.

Other feelings that people often have are listed below. Put a circle around the ones you have felt. If you don't know what a particular feeling is, ask an adult to explain it to you.

comfortable   **frustrated**   *anxious*   jealous

guilty

lonely   CONFUSED   **silly**

disappointed

excited   embarrassed

Objective: To give children a chance to name other feelings that haven't been identified or discussed.

Can you think of any other feelings? Write them on the lines below:

_____   _____   _____

_____   _____   _____

2. accept your feelings.

It is always OK to have or to feel a feeling. Feeling different feelings is normal. Experiencing feelings is your right. It is a part of being human. Sometimes other people will try to tell you not to feel a certain way. Someone might say, "Don't be sad," or "You shouldn't be angry." Usually when this happens, it means that the other person is uncomfortable with your feeling. Even if he or she is uncomfortable, you still have a right to what you are feeling.

3. express your feelings.

Objective: To help children differentiate between safe and unsafe ways of expressing feelings.

Just as you have a right to have your feelings, you also have a right to express them or let them out. Keeping feelings stuffed inside can make you uncomfortable or feel as if you're going to burst. Letting feelings out helps you to feel better.

When you let feelings out, it is very important to make sure you do it in a safe way. A safe way is one which doesn't hurt you and doesn't hurt anyone else either.

Following is a list of ways to let out feelings. Think about what might happen if you let out your feelings in each of these ways. Decide if each suggestion is a safe way or an unsafe way. To help you decide, ask yourself if it would hurt you or if it would hurt anyone else.

1. **Let out your anger by swinging a baseball bat around in your room.**

   Safe?_____ Unsafe?_____

2. **Let out your anger by playing baseball at the park.**

   Safe? _____ Unsafe? _____

3. **Let out your love by giving your newborn pet kitten a tight squeeze.**

   Safe?_____ Unsafe?_____

4. **Let out your love by giving your newborn pet kitten a gentle caress.**

   Safe?_____ Unsafe?_____

5. **Let out your excitement by pushing your friend into the pool.**

   Safe?_____ Unsafe?_____

6. **Let out your excitement by jumping into the swimming pool yourself.**

    Safe?_____ Unsafe?_____

7. **Let out your sadness by packing a suitcase and running away from home.**

    Safe?_____ Unsafe?_____

8. **Let out your sadness by cuddling with your teddy bear.**

    Safe?_____ Unsafe?_____

4. decide what you need to feel better.

Once you know what you are feeling, have accepted the feeling, and have let it out, you may still need some care to help yourself get over the problem. Sometimes you may be able to give yourself this care, and sometimes you may need to ask someone else to care for you.

Dealing with your feelings and expressing them in a safe way is a coping skill. It is a way to take care of yourself when you have a problem. It is a way of taking care of yourself on the inside.

On the next pages, you will find a number of stories about kids who need help with dealing with feelings. You can help these children by: 1) Labeling their feelings; 2) Telling them it's OK to feel them; 3) Suggesting safe ways to express their feelings; and 4) Deciding what kind of care they need.

After you finish these stories, you will be asked to think about your own experiences dealing with feelings. As you answer the questions, you can use what you know about dealing with feelings to help yourself.

DEAL WITH YOUR FEELINGS

Objective: To give children hands-on practice in learning recognition of feelings, acceptance of feelings, and safe methods for expressing feelings; and a chance to apply that knowledge to their own lives.

Ryan was walking through the lunch line in school. He put a cheeseburger, potato chips, and milk on his tray. When he walked over to join his friends at the table, he slipped on a wet spot on the floor and fell. His tray and burger went flying, and the milk spilled all over him. All the kids in the cafeteria looked at him and started laughing. Ryan wished he could just sink into the floor and disappear.

Help Ryan by:

1) Labeling his feelings: _____

_____

2) Telling him it's OK to feel this way: _____

_____

3) Suggesting a safe way for him to express his feelings: _____

Karin and her friend, Tammy, were in Karin's room playing Monopoly®. They heard a knock on the door, but when Karin got up and opened it, no one was there. A few minutes later it happened again. And then again. The last time, Karin heard some giggles and saw her little brother running down the hall. Karin doesn't like being bothered like that. She felt like throwing the Monopoly® board at her brother.

Help Karin by:

1) Labeling her feelings: _____

_____

2) Telling her that it's OK to feel this way: _____

_____

3) Suggesting a safe way for her to express her feelings: _____

_____

4) Deciding what she needs to feel better: _____

_____

When Bobby was six, he got a puppy for his birthday. He named the puppy Jibby, and let him sleep at the foot of his bed each night. Bobby fed Jibby every morning before school and played with him every afternoon. One day when Bobby got home from school, his mother asked him to sit next to her on the couch. She told Bobby that Jibby had been hit by a car and died. Bobby didn't want to believe it. He felt like someone had punched him in the stomach.

Help Bobby by:

1) Labeling his feelings: _____

_____

2) Telling him it's OK to feel this way: _____

_____

3) Suggesting a safe way for him to express his feelings: _____

_____

4) Deciding what he needs to feel better: _____

_____

O ne morning Lea woke up with a toothache. It hurt so much that she couldn't even eat her breakfast. Lea's mom called the dentist and made an appointment for that afternoon. Mom would come pick her up from school early and drive her to the dentist's office. Mom said she probably had a cavity, and the dentist would have to put in a filling. All day long, Lea had trouble concentrating in school. She just kept thinking about the dentist and wondering what he was going to do. She wondered if he would use a giant drill and if it would hurt even more than her toothache.

Help Lea by:

1) Labeling her feelings: _____

_____

2) Telling her it's OK to feel this way: _____

_____

3) Suggesting a safe way for her to express her feelings: _____

_____

4) Deciding what she needs to feel better: _____

_____

Meggie's grandma was one of her favorite people. She played Checkers with Meggie, watched scary movies with her, and baked special cakes on her birthday. One day Grandma had a heart attack and had to be rushed to the hospital. The doctor said that she was going to get better but that it would take a while for her to recover, and she would have to take things a little slower from now on. Meggie wanted her grandmother to be better right away. She wanted her to be healthy.

Help Meggie by:

1) Labeling her feelings: _____

_____

2) Telling her it's OK to feel this way: _____

_____

3) Suggesting a safe way for her to express her feelings: _____

_____

4) Deciding what she needs to feel better: _____

_____

DEAL WITH YOUR FEELINGS

Bernie is the goalie on his school soccer team. His best friend, Ted, is on the team, too. Bernie and Ted practice with the team three times a week after school. They compete with other schools on Friday afternoons. When their team was in the play-offs, Bernie and Ted practiced every day. They were sure that they would win the championship, and they planned a big party for after the match. But instead, their team lost the game by one point. Bernie and Ted felt like quitting the soccer team.

Help Bernie and Ted by:

1) Labeling their feelings: _____

_____

2) Telling them it's OK to feel this way: _____

_____

3) Suggesting a safe way for them to express their feelings: _____

_____

4) Deciding what they need to feel better: _____

_____

Jillian was playing at her friend Holly's house after dinner. They were making a huge tent with all of the blankets and sheets from Holly's mom's linen closet. Holly's mom said that Jillian could spend the night, and the girls could sleep in their tent. But when Jillian called her parents to ask permission, they said no, because it was a school night. Jillian hung up the phone and felt like never going home. Or maybe she would go home and behave so badly that her parents would beg her to go back to Holly's house.

Help Jillian by:

1) Labeling her feelings: _____

_____

2) Telling her it's OK to feel this way: _____

_____

3) Suggesting a safe way for her to express her feelings: _____

_____

4) Deciding what she needs to feel better: _____

_____

Matthew's parents had never gotten along very well. Matthew could hear them fighting downstairs after he went to bed at night. They would yell for awhile, and then one of them would leave the house, slamming the front door so hard he could feel the whole house shake. One night Matthew didn't hear any yelling, only talking. The next day his parents told him that his dad was moving out for awhile. This time it was Matthew who ran out of the house and slammed the door. He didn't know where he was going to go; he just knew that he wanted to get away.

Help Matthew by:

1) Labeling his feelings: _____

_____

2) Telling him it's OK to feel this way: _____

_____

3) Suggesting a safe way for him to deal with his feelings: _____

_____

4) Deciding what he needs to feel better: _____

_____

DEAL WITH YOUR FEELINGS

Write about something that happened to you recently where you had to deal with your feelings: _____

_____

_____

    Help yourself by:

    1) Labeling your feelings: _____

_____

    2) Telling yourself it's OK to feel this way: _____

_____

    3) Suggesting a safe way for you to deal with your feelings: _____

_____

    4) Deciding what you need to feel better: _____

_____

Now, write about something that might happen to you in the future where you will have to deal with your feelings: _____

_____

_____

    Help yourself ahead of time by:

    1) Labeling what you might feel when this happens: _____

_____

    2) Telling yourself it will be OK to feel this way: _____

_____

3) Suggesting a safe way for you to deal with your feelings: _____

_____

4) Deciding what you will need to feel better: _____

_____

CONGRATULATIONS! You have learned about how to deal with feelings, and you have shown that you know how to use this Coping Skill. This is a way of taking care of yourself on the inside. **GREAT JOB!**

COPING SKILL 2:

ADJUST YOUR ATTITUDE

Coping Skill #1 involved working with your feelings. Coping Skill #2 involves working with your brain. Our brains are what we use to think, and the way that we think affects the way we feel.

There is an old story that grown-ups like to tell about two people and a glass of water. This story helps us to understand how what we think affects what we feel. The story goes something like this:

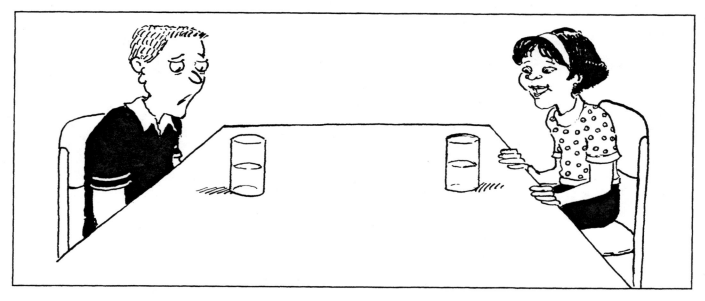

One day two friends went for a walk. It was a hot day, the sun was shining, and the friends walked for quite a while. When they were almost home, they were feeling very thirsty. They were looking forward to having something to drink.

When they got home, they found that all there was to drink was a half glass of water for each of them. When the first friend saw her half glass of water, a big smile appeared on her face, and she said, "Oh, good! My glass of water is half full!" When the second friend saw his half glass of water, he frowned and said, "Oh, no! My glass of water is half empty!"

Objective: To give children a chance to actively think about the connection between thoughts and feelings.

Both friends had exactly the same amount of water—a half glass. But one friend was happy, and one friend was sad. Do you know why they felt different? Write your answer here:

_____

_____

_____

_____

_____

The friends felt differently about the amount of water because they were thinking about it in different ways. What might the happy friend have been thinking? Write your answer here:

_____

_____

_____

_____

What might the sad friend have been thinking? Write your answer here:

_____

_____

_____

Sometimes it may seem that we don't have any control over our feelings; they seem to just "come over us." Or, we may think that someone or something can make us feel one way or another. We say things like, "That story made me cry," or "He makes me so mad."

But when we understand the story of the glass of water, we realize that no situation or person can make us feel anything. Our feelings do not come from outside of us. They come from inside of us, and they are directly determined by what we think. That means that if we change the way we think, our feelings will change, too.

Objective: To give children practice in changing negative thoughts to positive thoughts.

Think about the glass of water. How could the sad friend change his thinking in order to change his feelings about how much water he had? What could he say to himself? Write your answer below:

_____

_____

_____

_____

Now you can see that our feelings come from our thoughts. The sad friend could take care of himself and make himself feel better by changing what he was thinking. He could use his brain to help himself feel happy instead of sad.

Adjusting your attitude and deciding the best way to think about something is a coping skill. It is a way of taking care of yourself when you have a problem. It is a way of taking care of yourself on the inside.

On the next pages, you will find a number of stories about kids who need to adjust their attitudes and think in the way that will help them the most. You can help each child by: 1) Identifying what they are probably thinking; and 2) Suggesting different ways they can think about their situation.

After you finish these stories, you will be asked to think about your own experiences with adjusting your attitude. As you answer the questions, you can use what you know about adjusting your attitude to help yourself.

Objective: To give children hands-on practice in learning how feelings are affected by thoughts, and how changing our attitude can help us to feel better; and a chance to apply that knowledge to their own lives.

Shannon and Janelle spent the afternoon at the beach with their friends. They had a great time swimming, playing softball, and enjoying a barbeque. When their dad came to pick them up, they didn't want to leave. They asked if they could stay longer, but their dad said no; this was the time they had agreed to leave. Shannon and Janelle were mad and complained to their father the whole way home.

Help Shannon and Janelle by:

1) Identifying what they are probably thinking: _____

_____

2) Suggesting a different way they might think about the situation: _____

_____

_____

Dan looked forward to his birthday all month. His dad took him and five of his friends roller blading at the indoor rink. Afterwards they went out for pizza and then to the video arcade. Dan had a great time, until he opened his gifts. His friends had each given him a present, but none of them were what he really wanted. He had been hoping for tickets to the pro-hockey play-offs, but he didn't get them. Dan was really disappointed, and ignored his friends for the rest of the day.

Help Dan by:

1) Identifying what he is probably thinking: _____

_____

2) Suggesting a different way he might think about the situation: _____

_____

Elizabeth was excited to go to her last dance class. The dance instructor was going to assign parts for the annual end-of-the-year show. Elizabeth was sure she would be chosen for the lead in "Sleeping Beauty." After all, she had been taking lessons longer than any of the other girls. But when the instructor read off the assignments, Elizabeth was shocked to hear that Marianne had been chosen for the lead. Elizabeth would have to play a supporting part. She couldn't understand how the instructor could have done this to her. If she couldn't play Sleeping Beauty, she didn't want to be in the show at all.

Help Elizabeth by:

1) Identifying what she is probably thinking: _____

_____

2) Suggesting a different way for her to think about the situation: _____

_____

_____

Natalie had always gotten good grades. But then her mother went back to work full time. That meant her mom got home later, was a little crabbier, and the family never ate dinner until 8 o'clock. Natalie hated coming home to an empty house after school, so she began hanging out at the park with her friends until dinner. When report cards came out, all of Natalie's grades had dropped. They were the lowest she had ever gotten. Natalie told her mother that it wasn't her fault, because the teachers never explained the assignments right, and sometimes they didn't even tell her when things were due.

Help Natalie by:

1) Identifying what she is probably thinking: _____

_____

2) Suggesting a different way of thinking about the situation: _____

_____

Logan arrived at Boy Scout camp along with about 30 boys from other troops. Since none of his friends had signed up to go to camp this year, Logan figured he would make some new friends. He hoped his tent partner would like to swim as much as he did. He wanted to win the team relay again this year. When Logan's counselor introduced him to his tent partner, Steve, Logan didn't know what to say. Steve was in a wheelchair. Logan felt very uncomfortable and very let down.

Help Logan by:

1) Identifying what he is probably thinking: _____

_____

2) Suggesting a different way of thinking about the situation: _____

_____

_____

ADJUST YOUR ATTITUDE

uring spring vacation, some of Jeff's friends were going on a special school trip to the state capital. The students and teachers would stay in a hotel, tour the city, and also have free time to themselves. Jeff really wanted to go on the trip, but his parents were taking him to visit his grandfather who lived on a farm. Jeff told his mom he wanted to spend his vacation with his friends, not a bunch of farm animals.

Help Jeff by:

1) Identifying what he is probably thinking: _____

_____

2) Suggesting a different way for him to think about the situation: _____

_____

_____

onathan was excited when he woke up on the first day of summer vacation. No more school! He was ready for fun. He and his friends planned to spend the day riding the bike trail near their houses. He grabbed a piece of toast and started out the front door, when he heard his dad call him back. His dad said that he couldn't go out until he had mowed the lawn. Jonathan was furious. The lawn would take him at least an hour! He wanted to leave now.

Help Jonathan by:

1) Identifying what he is probably thinking: _____

_____

2) Suggesting a different way for him to think about the situation: _____

_____

_____

Lexie didn't know anyone in her new neighborhood. Her mom had encouraged her to go outside and meet some kids, but the first time she'd walked up to a group of girls, she heard them all laughing. She turned around and went right back home. She hadn't tried again. She just watched from her window while the other kids played outside. Lexie was lonely and wanted to make friends, but it didn't seem like anyone wanted to be friends with her.

Help Lexie by:

1) Identifying what she is probably thinking:

_____

_____

_____

_____

2) Suggesting a different way for her to think about the situation: _____

_____

Write about something that happened to you recently where you could have

adjusted your attitude to make things better: _____

_____

_____

_____

_____

_____

_____

Help yourself by:

1) Identifying what you were thinking: _____

_____

2) Suggesting a different way you could have thought about the situation:

_____

_____

Now, write about something that might happen to you in the future where adjusting

your attitude could help you out: _____

_____

_____

Help yourself ahead of time by:

1) Identifying what you might think when this happens: _____

_____

2) Suggesting a different way for you to think about the situation: _____

_____

_____

CONGRATULATIONS! You have learned about how to adjust your attitude, and you have shown that you know how to use this Coping Skill. This is a way of taking care of yourself on the inside. **WAY TO GO!**

COPING SKILL 3:

DISCOVER YOUR CHOICES

Sometimes when we are stuck in a problem situation, it seems that no matter how hard we try, we can't change things in any way. If we look harder, however, we will find that we always have some kind of choice in making things better for ourselves.

In every problem situation, there are always things we can't change and things we can change. As we learned with Coping Skill #2 (Adjusting Your Attitude), if nothing else, we can always change the way we think about something.

Coping Skill #3 is about seeing our choices and putting our energy toward changing the things that can be changed.

It involves three steps:

1. Look carefully at your problem.

2. Discover the things you can't change and the things you can change.

3. Choose something you can change and work on making it better.

1. Look carefully at your problem.

Sometimes it is hard to see the things that we can change right away. But a problem can be like a puzzle—the longer and harder you look, the more answers you will find.

Objective: To give children hands-on experience in looking closely at something to discover its components, and to understand that careful observation can reveal more than just a first glance.

Look at the picture below. This family looks unhappy because everyone has lost something in this room. Can you find what each person has lost? Who do you think lost what? Can you find all 10 things that are lost? (Keys, doll, truck, glove, purse, sock, boots, books, pet rabbit and toy mouse).

Objective: To help children understand that careful observation can reveal more than just at first glance.

Here is another picture puzzle. There are two ways of looking at this picture. Looking at it one way, we may call it a picture of a vase. But, looking at it from another way, we may call it a picture of two faces. Can you see both pictures?

With real life problems, things are often like these picture puzzles: At first you may see things only one way; but if you look a little harder, you will be able to discover more. Looking more carefully at our problems can help us to find things we can change about them. Then we can make a choice as to what we want to change. And, finally, we can take action to do it.

2. discover the things you can't change and the things you can change.

There are so many things that happen to us every day, and there are always things that we can and cannot change about them.

When your mother wakes you up in the morning, you can't change the fact that you have to go to school, but you can decide what clothes you want to wear, what you want to eat for breakfast, and whether you will be happy or grumpy that day.

When you get to school, you can't change what grade you are in or who your teacher is, but you can decide who you will be friends with, how hard you will work, and what kind of activities you will join.

Right now you are in a room somewhere reading this book. What can't you change about this situation? What can you change? Write your answers below.

Objective: To give children practice in identifying things that they can't change.

Things I can't change: _____

_____

_____

_____

Objective: To give children practice in identifying things that they can change.

Things I can change: _____

_____

_____

_____

Remember, one thing that you can always change is the way you think about things.

3. Choose something that you can change and work on making it better.

Taking action is the final step. Even if you know what you can change, if you don't work on doing it, nothing will be any different.

Many people are good at knowing what is wrong with a situation, but they don't use their energy to do anything about it. That doesn't make things any better for them.

Discovering what you can change and then doing something to make it better is a coping skill. It is a way of taking care of yourself when you have a problem. It is a way of taking care of yourself on the inside.

On the next pages, you will find stories about kids who need to discover their choices about what they can change and then take action to do it. You can help each child by: 1) Looking carefully at their problem; 2) Discovering the things that they can and cannot change; and 3) Suggesting what they can do to work on making things better.

After you finish these stories, you will be asked to think about your own experiences with things you can and cannot change. As you answer the questions, you can use what you know about discovering your choices to help yourself.

Objective: To give children hands-on experience in learning that every situation contains things that can be changed and things that cannot be changed, and that if we discover the things that can be changed and work toward doing so, we can improve our situations; and a chance to apply that knowledge to their own lives.

Chloe was mad. Her mom hadn't done the laundry the day before, and Chloe didn't have anything to wear to school. Well, there were a couple of things, but not the clothes that she wanted. She stared at her closet and grumbled. This always happened when her mom spent the day with her friends. She never got home in time to do the laundry. Then Chloe was stuck with nothing to wear. She wished she had a maid. Or a mom who didn't have friends. Or more clothes.

Help Chloe by:

1) Listing some of the things she can't change: _____

_____

2) Listing some of the things she can change: _____

_____

3) Suggesting something she could work on to make things better: _____

_____

Anna wouldn't come out of her room. Her mom's boyfriend, Sam, was coming for dinner. Anna didn't want to have dinner with Sam. She didn't want him in their house. She didn't want her mom to like him. Anna wanted her mom to like her dad. She wanted her mom and dad to get back together again and have her dad move back home and have everything the way it used to be. Anna hated her mom and dad being divorced. Even if Sam was nice to her and her mom, he still wasn't her dad.

Help Anna by:

1) Listing some of the things she can't change: _____

_____

2) Listing some of the things she can change: _____

_____

3) Suggesting something she could work on to make things better: _____

_____

Joey hated walking to school. Every time he passed the older kids waiting for their bus, they teased him and called him names. Sometimes they ran after him, just to scare him. Every morning Joey told his mom that he didn't want to go to school, but she always said that he had to. Joey was afraid of those kids because they were twice as big as him and twice as strong. He figured they could beat him up in a minute. He wished he didn't have to go to school at all.

Help Joey by:

1) Listing some of the things he

can't change: _____

_____

2) Listing some of the things he can change: _____

_____

3) Suggesting something he could work on to make things better: _____

_____

Emily's timing couldn't have been worse. She had sprained her ankle the day before the school track meet. Emily was the best runner in her grade, and she was signed up for three different races. Her parents had bought her new track shoes that she had been breaking in all week. Her whole family had planned to come to the meet, and there was a party at school afterwards. Now Emily felt that everything was ruined. She decided not to go to the meet at all.

Help Emily by:

1) Listing some of the things she can't change: _____

_____

2) Listing some of the things she can change: _____

_____

3) Suggesting something she could work on to make things better: _____

_____

Terry had done it again. He had lost his homework paper. This was the fourth time this month that he had done his homework and then lost it. Both his teacher and his mom were upset with him, and Terry was upset with himself, too. He didn't know why his papers kept disappearing. He couldn't find them in his room because it was pretty messy. He couldn't find them in his book bag because he had left that on the bus and had never gotten a new one. He couldn't find them in his locker because his lock had been stolen and he never kept anything in there anymore.

Help Terry by:

1) Listing some of the things he can't change: _____

_____

2) Listing some of the things he can change: _____

_____

3) Suggesting something he could work on to make things better: _____

_____

One of David's friends found a pack of cigarettes and passed them out after school. Some of the kids were smoking and wanted David to try it, but he didn't want to. At first he said no, but they kept bothering him and then called him a sissy because he wouldn't try. Finally David gave in and took a drag from the cigarette. He hated the smell and the taste, and he coughed a lot. When he got home, he went into his room and closed the door. David felt sick and also stupid for giving in to his friends. He didn't want to smoke. His aunt had died from lung cancer last year. He was mad at himself and wished he hadn't done it.

Help David by:

1) Listing some of the things he can't change: _____

_____

2) Listing some of the things he can change: _____

_____

3) Suggesting something he could work on to make things better: _____

_____

_____

Alyssa felt like a giant. She was the biggest kid in her school. She was taller than all the other girls, and there were only two boys whom she didn't tower over. She had a hard time finding clothes to fit in the styles she liked and was embarrassed when people commented on her height, even when they were being nice. Alyssa got good grades and had a lot of friends, but she was sad a lot of the time because she felt so different from the other kids.

Help Alyssa by:

1) Listing some of the things she can't change: _____

_____

2) Listing some of the things she can change: _____

_____

3) Suggesting something she could work on to make things better: _____

_____

_____

Luke was bored. His best friend, Craig, was at summer camp. His older brother had gotten a job as a lifeguard and was working all day. Luke had seen every TV rerun twice already. He wished he could be at camp with Craig. He didn't like any of the other kids in the neighborhood. Well, the ones he knew, anyway. He wished he were old enough to have a job. If he had any money of his own, he could go to the mall. He thought about the long summer stretching ahead and only felt more bored.

Help Luke by:

1) Listing some of the things he can't change: _____

_____

2) Listing some of the things he can change: _____

_____

3) Suggesting something he could work on to make things better: _____

_____

_____

Write about something that happened to you recently where you could have looked for your choices and made things better for yourself:

_____

_____

Help yourself by:

1) Listing some of the things you couldn't change: _____

_____

2) Listing some of the things you could have changed: _____

_____

3) Suggesting something you could have worked on to make things better:

_____

Now, write about something that might happen to you in the future where discovering your choices could help you out: _____

_____

_____

_____

Help yourself ahead of time by:

1) Listing some of the things you won't be able to change: _____

_____

2) Listing some of the things you will be able to change: _____

_____

3) Suggesting something you may be able to work on to make things better:

_____

_____

CONGRATULATIONS! You have learned about how to discover your choices, and you have shown that you know how to use this Coping Skill. This is a way of taking care of yourself on the inside. **GOOD JOB!**

COPING SKILL 4:

ACCEPT IMPERFECTION

Did you know that there is one thing that is the same about every person you meet?

No matter who they are, no matter what their age is, no matter where they live, or what their family is like, or where they go to school, or what their job is, they are all the same in one way: They all make mistakes.

Even if they are very smart and try very hard, every single person in the world makes a mistake at one time or another. That is because we are human beings, and human beings are imperfect. We use the word "perfect" to mean something that is very, very good, but really, there is no one or nothing that is completely without a flaw.

Think of three people you know. Can you think of a mistake they have each made at some time? Write their names and mistakes below:

Objective: To help children understand that everyone makes mistakes.

1) Name: _____

   Mistake: _____

2) Name: _____

   Mistake: _____

3) Name: _____

   Mistake: _____

ACCEPT IMPERFECTION

Objective: To help children accept that they are included in the population of "everyone" who makes mistakes.

Can you think of a mistake you made at some time? Write it here: _____

_____

_____

No one sets out to make mistakes on purpose. And sometimes it can feel very frustrating when we do make a mistake. But, no matter how careful we are, we can never be perfect. That is why there are erasers on pencils!

It usually feels good when we succeed at something. Can you think of three things that you do well? Write them here:

Objective: To help raise self-esteem.

1) _____

2) _____

3) _____

Even though you do these things well, at some time or another you might make a mistake while you are doing them.

ACCEPT IMPERFECTION

When that happens, instead of getting too upset, you can accept imperfection by:

1) Reminding yourself that no one and nothing is perfect.

2) Thinking of a way to adjust your attitude or discover your choices to make things better.

Just as people aren't perfect, situations aren't perfect either. Remembering this keeps us from being too disappointed or upset when things don't go exactly the way we would like.

Objective: To help children relate to the concept of imperfect situations.

Can you think of a time when you were disappointed because something didn't happen the way you wanted it to?

Write about it here: _____

_____

_____

When things don't go the way you'd planned, it's OK to feel disappointed. But instead of letting it ruin everything else for you, you can take care of yourself by accepting it, and then use some other coping skills to adjust your attitude or discover your choices and change what you can.

Accepting imperfection can help to keep you from feeling disappointed or being angry with yourself or other people when things go wrong. This is a Coping Skill. It is a way of taking care of yourself when you have a problem. It is a way of taking care of yourself on the inside.

On the next pages, you will find a number of stories about kids who need to accept imperfection. You can help them by: 1) Reminding them that no one and nothing is
perfect; 2) Suggesting a way to adjust their attitude or discover their choices to make things better.

After you finish these stories, you will be asked to think about your own experiences with accepting imperfection. As you answer the questions, you can use what you know about changing your thinking or discovering your choices to help yourself.

ACCEPT IMPERFECTION

Objective: To give children hands-on experience in learning that imperfection is a natural and unavoidable part of life, and by adjusting our attitude or discovering our choices we can better cope with mistakes and disappointments; and a chance to apply that knowledge to their own lives.

Rick had been working all semester to bring up his math grade. Math was the hardest subject for him, and he had to spend a lot of extra time with his homework in order to understand the assignments and work the problems correctly. Finally, after trying his hardest, he had almost brought his grade up from a D to a B. If he got a B in math, he would have all Bs on his report card. That would be the best he had ever done. When the day came for the final test, Rick was prepared. But the last problem on the test was difficult. Rick didn't know how to solve it. He felt awful when he got a C on the test and a C on his report card.

Help Rick by:

1) Reminding him that no one and nothing is perfect: _____

_____

2) Suggesting a way for him to adjust his attitude to make things better:

_____

_____

Melanie was trying out for the fall play at school. At the audition, she was asked to sing a song from the play and to recite some of the lines from memory. Melanie sang the song beautifully, but when she tried to remember the lines, her mind went blank. She tried to start over, but that made her even more nervous, and she couldn't remember a thing. She could feel her face growing red with embarrassment. As she walked off the stage, she decided she would never try out for a play again.

Help Melanie by:

1) Reminding her that no one or nothing is perfect: _____

_____

2) Suggesting a way for her to adjust her attitude or discover her choices to make things

better: _____

_____

Kaitlin was making her mother a surprise for her birthday. She was baking her a birthday cake from scratch. She had looked in the cookbook and had all the ingredients. She woke up early on her mother's birthday and sneaked quietly down to the kitchen to bake the cake. She measured and mixed and put everything in the oven. She had frosting ready for when the cake was done. But when she opened the oven door, her face fell. The cake was only one inch high! Then she saw the can of baking powder on the counter and realized she had forgotten to add it so the cake would rise. Kaitlin could hear her mother coming down the stairs. She felt terrible.

Help Kaitlin by:

1) Reminding her that no one and nothing is perfect: _____

_____

2) Suggesting a way for her to adjust her attitude or discover choices to make things better:

_____

Michael's class was planning a picnic by the lake on the last day of school. There would be food and games, and each student would get an award for trying his best in school. All the kids were looking forward to the celebration. On the day of the picnic, Michael woke up to thunder and lightning. It was raining hard. The principal wouldn't let the kids go to the lake; they had to have their picnic in the gym instead. Michael and his friends were all disappointed. What rotten luck!

Help Michael by:

1) Reminding him that no one and nothing is perfect: _____

_____

2) Suggesting a way for him to adjust his attitude or discover choices to make things better:

_____

_____

Sean and his dad loved watching football together. They were looking forward to the Super Bowl but realized that Sean's little sister's music recital was on the same day. They decided to tape the game so they could watch it after the recital. Sean set the video recorder, and they went to the recital. When Sean and his dad sat down later to watch the recorded game, they found a different show on the tape instead. They couldn't figure what went wrong, until Sean realized that he had set the recorder for the wrong channel. They had missed the whole Super Bowl.

Help Sean by:

1) Reminding him that no one and nothing is perfect: _____

_____

2) Suggesting a way for him to adjust his attitude or discover choices to make things better:

_____

_____

_____

ACCEPT IMPERFECTION

Tyler was playing basketball with his friend, Greg, in the street. One time as Tyler was throwing the ball, he tried putting a little spin on it. To his surprise, the ball went harder and farther than he had expected, and Greg missed it. The ball hit the neighbor's car and bent its antenna.

Help Tyler by:

1) Reminding him that no one and nothing is perfect: _____

_____

2) Suggesting a way that he could adjust his attitude or discover choices to make things better:

_____

_____

Merilee was eating dinner at Jason's house. She had never met his family before, and she was a little nervous. Merilee liked Jason a lot. He was friendly and had a nice smile, and sometimes he walked her home from school. She was trying to use her best manners during dinner, but when she reached across the table to pass Jason's mother the beans, her elbow hit her glass and sent her milk flying. There was milk on her plate, on her shirt, and worst of all, on Jason's mother.

Help Merilee by:

1) Reminding her that no one and nothing is perfect: _____

_____

2) Suggesting a way for her to adjust her attitude or discover choices to make things better:

_____

Carly's friend, Jeanne, invited her to spend the weekend camping with her family. Carly packed games and books and marshmallows to roast and thought about the fun she would have being with Jeanne for a whole weekend. They could go hiking and swimming and stay up late. The first day was fun, but the second day Jeanne seemed to wake up in a bad mood. She was moody and quiet and hardly talked to Carly. Carly ended up spending more time with Jeanne's younger sister on the second day than she did with Jeanne. They went hiking and swimming, but Jeanne stayed grumpy the whole day.

Help Carly by:

1) Reminding her that no one and nothing is perfect: _____

_____

2) Suggesting a way for her to adjust her attitude or discover choices to make things better:

_____

_____

ACCEPT IMPERFECTION

Write about something that happened to you recently where accepting imperfection would have made things easier for you: _____

_____

_____

Help yourself by:

1) Reminding yourself that no one or nothing is perfect: _____

_____

2) Suggesting a way that you could have adjusted your attitude or discovered your choices to make things better: _____

_____

Now, write about something that might happen to you in the future where accepting imperfection could help you out: _____

_____

_____

Help yourself by:

1) Reminding yourself that no one or nothing is perfect: _____

_____

2) Suggesting a way that you might be able to adjust your attitude or discover your choices to make things better: _____

_____

CONGRATULATIONS! You have learned about how to accept imperfection, and you have shown that you know how to use this Coping Skill. This is a way of taking care of yourself on the inside. **NICE JOB!**

COPING SKILL 5:

GIVE YOURSELF A BREAK

Anything that you do in life uses your energy. Riding your bike uses energy, doing your homework uses energy, playing with your friends uses energy, reading this book uses energy.

Objective: To help children understand the concept of using up energy.

Can you think of some other activities that use your energy? Write them here:

_____

_____

_____

_____

_____

Energy isn't limitless. At some point we run out of it, just like a car runs out of gas. When a car runs out of gas, it's time to stop and refuel. When we run out of physical energy, it's time to stop and refuel ourselves by sleeping or eating. When we run out of emotional or mental energy, it's time to stop and take a break.

Refueling our physical bodies is a way of taking care of ourselves on the outside. We use up physical energy by moving around. When our bodies run out of energy, we may notice it by feeling tired or hungry. Then we take care of ourselves by sleeping or eating.

We use up emotional and mental energy by feeling and thinking. When we run out, we may notice it by feeling crabby or impatient, by finding it hard to concentrate, or by making a lot of mistakes. We can take care of ourselves then by taking a break. This is a way of taking care of ourselves on the inside. This is Coping Skill #5.

Objective: To give children a chance to input their own ideas, helping to raise self-esteem.

What does it mean to take a break? Do you have a guess? Write it here:

_____

_____

_____

_____

GIVE YOURSELF A BREAK

Objective: To help children actively think about actual ways to take breaks.

When someone takes a break, it means they make a change in what they are doing for awhile. If you are working very hard on a homework problem, and have been working at it for a very long time, you might feel yourself getting mentally tired. Maybe you're getting a little frustrated, or maybe your head is starting to feel light—or heavy. These are your signals that it is time to take a break. Can you think of some ways to do that? Write your ideas here: _____

_____

_____

_____

There are a number of ways that we can take breaks that help us refuel with emotional and mental energy. Here are some ideas:

change your activity	**take a deep breath**	**look out the window**
stretch your body	**take a walk**	**take a nap**
have a drink of water	**listen to some music**	**talk to a friend**

Objective: To help children stretch their imaginations and use creative thinking skills.

Can you think of some other ways to take a break? Write your ideas here:

_____

_____

_____

Usually the best ways to take a break involve some kind of relaxation. When we are tense or stressed, life tends to seem more difficult. Whatever we are trying to do may seem harder than usual. If we can relax ourselves at these times, we will find problems easier to solve because we have more emotional and mental energy to put towards them. Taking a break and relaxing in some way will help us recharge our emotional and mental energy.

"Bringing yourself to a peaceful state" is one way to take a break. It involves relaxing your mind and body. It helps you to feel peaceful on the inside instead of tense or anxious. Try the following exercise. You may want to ask someone to read it to you as you try it. It will be the most helpful if it's read slowly and calmly.

Sit comfortably in a chair. Close your eyes. Take a deep breath. Think of all the air that is coming inside your body as Relaxing Air. Every time you breathe and bring some of this Relaxing Air into your body, it moves around inside you and releases the tension. Each time you breathe, the Relaxing Air comes in, and you feel more and more peaceful.

Keeping your eyes closed, picture the Relaxing Air as it moves through all the parts of your body. Picture Relaxing Air moving up to your head, and relaxing your face, and your brain, and the back of your neck. Now see the Relaxing Air moving down to your shoulders, relaxing your back and your arms, and your hands and your fingers.

Now the Relaxing Air is moving through your chest and your stomach and down to your hips. Each body part that it moves through immediately feels more relaxed. Now it is moving through your legs and your knees and down to your ankles, your feet, and your toes.

The Relaxing Air has moved through your whole body, and you feel very peaceful inside. In your mind, you picture yourself in your favorite place, doing your favorite activity. You are happy and calm. Enjoy that picture for a little while. Now pay attention again to the chair you are sitting in, and when you are ready, open your eyes.

You can use the Relaxing Air exercise when you feel tense. It is a good way to take a break, because it only takes a few minutes and you don't need any equipment! Someone else can talk you through it, or you can do it by yourself.

Giving yourself a break by changing your activity for awhile or relaxing is a Coping Skill. It is a way to take care of yourself when you have a problem. It is a way of taking care of yourself on the inside.

On the next pages, you will find a number of stories about kids who need to give themselves a break. You can help them each by: 1) Pointing out why they need a break; and 2) Suggesting a way for them to take one.

After you finish these stories, you will be asked to think about your own experiences with giving yourself a break. As you answer the questions, you can use what you know about relaxing and changing your activity to help yourself.

Objective: To give children hands-on experience in learning that relaxing and taking breaks can help to renew our energy, to learn specific techniques to this end, and a chance to apply that knowledge to their own lives.

Jeremy had four tests to take during the last week of school: in science, math, English, and social studies. He planned to study all day on Sunday, so he got up early and opened his books. By 10 o'clock he had put in two hours, and he was starting to fidget. His back hurt, his eyes were blurring a little, and it was getting harder to understand what he was reading. He wanted to quit, but he hadn't even opened his math, English, or social studies books yet. He wanted to get good grades on these tests.

Help Jeremy by:

1) Pointing out why he needs to take a break: _____

_____

2) Suggesting a way that he could take one: _____

_____

Ally was swamped, as usual. Her mom was working two jobs now, which left Ally in charge of the house and her younger brother and sister. She picked them up at day care after school and came home to a pile of dirty dishes, two loads of laundry, and her own homework which was due the next day. The kids were crying for dinner, so she gave them peanut butter sandwiches while she put in a load of laundry and tried to start her homework. In a few minutes they were done—with peanut butter all over themselves and their clothes. Ally knew she would have to bathe them, wash their clothes, and clean up the house before her mom got home. And what about her homework? She wanted to cry or scream, or both.

Help Ally by:

1) Pointing out why she needs to take a break: _____

_____

2) Suggesting a way that she could take one: _____

_____

Eric wanted to make the basketball team this year. He had tried out last year, but the coach said he wasn't fast enough. So this year Eric had been running a few miles every day after school. Tryouts were next week, and he really wanted to get on the team. He decided to double his efforts for the next few days and run twice as far. The first day he was winded, but he made one extra mile. The second day he was going to go for two extra, but after the first mile he started feeling tired. The muscles in his legs were hurting, and he was really thirsty. He really wanted to make the team, but he didn't know if he could run any farther.

Help Eric by:

1) Pointing out why he needs to take a break: _____

_____

2) Suggesting a way that he could take one: _____

_____

Lauren hadn't seen her mom in a long time. She had been living with her grandparents for several years, because her mom had a drinking problem and wasn't able to take care of her. She didn't know where her dad was. Now Lauren's mom was coming to visit. She hadn't had any alcohol in six months. Lauren had pictures of her mom, and remembered her a little bit, but she didn't know what it would be like to be with her again. As Lauren was getting dressed, she noticed her muscles were more tense than usual, and she was shaking a little. Her heart was pounding fast, and she felt a little dizzy in her head. Lauren was scared of what would happen with her mom and of what was happening to her right then.

Help Lauren by:

1) Pointing out why she needs to take a break: _____

_____

2) Suggesting a way that she could take one: _____

_____

_____

Molly was spending the day at Jessica's house while her parents went to a wedding. She and Jessica didn't see each other very often because they went to different schools, so they were thrilled to have the whole day together. The first thing they did was have pancakes for breakfast. Then they roller skated, worked a jigsaw puzzle, built a fort, had lunch, played with dolls, and walked to the store and back. When they sat down to watch TV, they started fighting. They couldn't agree on which show to watch. "I'm getting tired of you!" Jessica said. Molly agreed, "I'm getting tired of you, too!"

Help Molly and Jessica by:

1) Pointing out why they need to take a break: _____

_____

2) Suggesting a way that they could take one: _____

_____

Adam woke up in the middle of the night and couldn't go back to sleep. He couldn't get his mind to relax. He was thinking about his parents fighting. They were fighting more and more since his dad lost his job. He worried about that, too. What would they do if his dad didn't find another job? How would they get money? He hadn't told his parents about the test he failed in school today, either. He didn't want them to have more to worry about or fight about. Adam was scared. He had to get up for school in two more hours. He tossed and turned and worried and couldn't go to sleep.

Help Adam by:

1) Pointing out why he needs to take a break: _____

_____

2) Suggesting a way that he could take one: _____

_____

_____

Joshua was learning to play guitar. He wanted to be good enough to join a band that some other kids at school had formed. But they had been playing for a couple of years, and he was just a beginner. They said they would listen to him tomorrow after school. He wanted to do his best. He had been practicing all afternoon. His fingertips were red and sore, and he was starting to make silly mistakes. That made him discouraged, and he felt he had to practice even longer.

Help Joshua by:

1) Pointing out why he needs to take a break: _____

_____

2) Suggesting a way that he could take one: _____

_____

_____

GIVE YOURSELF A BREAK

Mark was furious. He sat and stared at the computer. He couldn't figure out why he couldn't get it to do what he wanted. He had spent the last 15 minutes trying to print out his English paper, but the stupid computer kept moving all the paragraphs over to the right side of the page. He couldn't turn in his paper like that. He had tried to read the computer manual, but it was hard to understand. He tried figuring it out himself, but it was only making things worse. He felt like putting his fist through the screen!

Help Mark by:

1) Pointing out why he needs to take a break: _____

_____

2) Suggesting a way that he could take one: _____

_____

_____

Write about something that happened to you recently where you would have benefitted from giving yourself a break: _____

_____

_____

Help yourself by:

1) Pointing out why you needed to take a break: _____

_____

2) Suggesting a way you could have taken one: _____

_____

Now, write about something that might happen to you in the future where taking a break could help you out: _____

_____

_____

Help yourself by:

1) Pointing out why you will need to take a break: _____

_____

2) Suggesting a way you might be able to take one: _____

_____

CONGRATULATIONS! You have learned about how to give yourself a break, and you have shown that you know how to use this Coping Skill. This is a way of taking care of yourself on the inside. **GOOD WORK!**

COPING SKILL 6:

TAKE ONE STEP AT A TIME

People who have many things to do or a lot of things to think about at one time can start to feel overwhelmed. Being overwhelmed means feeling pressured and maybe a little frightened that we can't handle everything. We might feel like we have to rush or do two or three things at once. Our time may feel "crowded," or our brain may feel "stretched."

Being overwhelmed can be so uncomfortable that we may have a hard time thinking about or doing even one thing. We may wish we could just "shut down" or run away.

When we start to feel this way, we can take care of ourselves by using Coping Skill #6: Taking Things One Step at a Time. This means that we stop trying to do everything at once, or think about everything at once, and we focus on only one activity or thought. This helps us to relax and concentrate, to feel less jumbled, and to focus on each thing clearly.

In the lines below, a number of words have all run together. Can you rewrite them, one at a time, so that the jumble is gone and each word can be seen clearly?

Objective: To give children practice in separating a whole into its parts.

catbirdbedmomringhouseflowerdogdadmilkball

_____ _____ _____ _____

_____ _____ _____ _____

You helped yourself to see the above words clearly by putting space between them and taking them one at a time. You can do the same thing when you have a lot of things to do or think about at the same time. Doing or thinking about them one at a time, with space between them, will help prevent you from becoming overwhelmed.

Putting things in order of importance can also help. Knowing what things need to be done or thought about first, second, and third lets you know what needs attention right away and what can wait until later.

When you wake up in the morning, you know there are many things that you will need to do that day. Write some of them here:

Objective: To help children apply ideas set forth to their own lives.

_____

_____

_____

Now, put the activities you wrote in order. Which needs to be done first, second, third, and so on?

Objective: To give children a chance to practice prioritizing.

1. _____

2. _____

3. _____

4. _____

TAKE ONE STEP AT A TIME

Taking things one step at a time can help you stay calm and confident and can prevent you from becoming overwhelmed. It is a coping skill. It is a way of taking care of yourself when you have a problem. It is a way of taking care of yourself on the inside.

On the next pages, you will find a number of stories about kids who need to slow down and take things one step at a time. You can help them by: 1) Identifying all of their thoughts or tasks; and 2) Putting them in the order in which they should be done.

After you finish these stories, you will be asked to think about your own experiences taking things one step at a time. As you answer the questions, you can use what you know about putting space between things and putting them in order of importance to help yourself.

Objective: To give children hands-on experience in breaking down and prioritizing tasks to keep from being overwhelmed, and a chance to apply that knowledge to their own lives.

Kiesha wanted to go to a movie with her friends at 2 o'clock. But before she could go, she had to make her bed and take a shower. She had some math homework left to do. Her mother had asked her to walk the dog, and she knew she still had to take out the garbage from the night before. She only had two hours to get everything done. It looked like rain outside, and her dog was crying at the door. She wondered if she would be able to finish it all in time.

Help Kiesha by:

1) Identifying all the things she needs to do: _____

_____

2) Putting them in order of importance for her:

1. _____

2. _____

3. _____

4. _____

5. _____

TAKE ONE STEP AT A TIME

Tom was baby-sitting his little brother while his mom was at the store. He heard the baby crying, so he went in to check on him. His brother had pulled off his wet diaper and was trying to climb out of his crib. As Tom went to get him, he heard the doorbell ring. He knew his mom was expecting a delivery. Then the phone rang, and just a second later he heard the buzzer signaling that the laundry was done. Everything was happening at once; Tom didn't know what to do.

Help Tom by:

1) Identifying all the things he needs to do: _____

_____

2) Putting them in order of importance for him:

1. _____

2. _____

3. _____

4. _____

Julia sat at the kitchen table and took all her books and papers out of her backpack. She had so much homework! There were assignments in three subjects, two tests to study for, and a research paper to write for English. It was Monday. Her spelling test was tomorrow; her history test was in two days. The math and reading assignments were due on Friday, and the assignment in her science workbook was due on Thursday.

Help Julia by:

1) Identifying all the things she needs to do: _____

_____

2) Putting them in order of importance for her:

1. _____   2. _____

3. _____   4. _____

5. _____   6. _____

Scott looked around his room. His mother had given him what seemed like an impossible task: cleaning his room. It had been a while since he had seen the floor. There were dirty clothes mixed with clean clothes; they needed to go in the hamper and in his closet. There was a can of pop stuck to his dresser, along with a half a bowl of cereal. There were comic books on his desk along with the homework papers he had started to sort last night. His bed was unmade, and the sheets needed to be changed. On top of everything was a layer of dust.

Help Scott by:

1) Identifying all the things he needs to do: _____

_____

2) Putting them in order of importance for him:

1. _____

2. _____

3. _____

4. _____

5. _____

6. _____

Ellyn planned to make her own Halloween costume this year. She was going to dress up as a baseball player. Her dad had said she could wear his old uniform from high school, but she would have to sew buttons on it and shorten the pants. A friend had said she could borrow his mitt and a baseball, but she'd have to go over to his house to pick them up. She had to find her mom's sewing box and also get some black make-up to put under her eyes. She only had a couple of days before Halloween, so she wanted to get started.

Help Ellyn by:

1) Identifying all the things she needs to do: _____

_____

2) Putting them in order of importance for her:

    1. _____

    2. _____

    3. _____

    4. _____

Kurt had been called into the principal's office. He was in trouble for getting in a fight on the playground the day before. He had pushed another boy and broken his glasses. Kurt owed him an apology and would have to earn money to pay for the glasses. He was also in trouble with his grades. He was failing two classes because he hadn't turned in his homework. Some of it he had done and had just left at home; some of it he hadn't finished yet. The principal told him he had a lot to work on if he didn't want to get suspended. Kurt knew that, but he didn't know if he could do it all. He had felt really down since his father's car accident, and he didn't seem to have any energy.

Help Kurt by:

1) Identifying all the things he needs to do: _____

_____

2) Putting them in order of importance for him:

    1. _____

    2. _____

    3. _____

    4. _____

Gerry had to write a report for English class. It had to be typed and put into a folder, and he had to design a cover for the folder. He had to pick a book to read, watch a movie about the same story, and write about how they were the same or different and which he liked better. He also had to have an outline of the report and note cards so he could give a presentation in front of the class. The project seemed huge when Gerry thought about all that work.

Help Gerry by:

1) Identifying all the things that he needs to do: _____

_____

2) Putting them in order of importance for him:

    1. _____

    2. _____

    3. _____

    4. _____

    5. _____

    6. _____

    7. _____

    8. _____

Gwen's mind was racing as she walked home from school. She had promised to bake something for the pep club bake sale tomorrow, and she had to decide on a topic for her science project by next week. She was trying to remember whether she had brought her gym suit home and where she had left her Spanish notebook. She wondered if she would go to camp this summer and if her mom would let her go to the beach for a week with her cousin. She had to remember to call her dad to tell him mom was working late, and she was supposed to order a pizza for dinner. Gwen felt like she was getting a headache.

Help Gwen by:

1) Identifying all the things she needs to do: _____

_____

2) Putting them in order of importance for her:

1. _____ 2. _____

3. _____ 4. _____

5. _____ 6. _____

7. _____ 8. _____

Write about something that happened to you recently where you would have benefitted

from taking one step at a time: _____

_____

_____

Help yourself by:

1) Identifying all the things that you needed to do: _____

_____

2) Putting them in order of importance:

   1. _____

   2. _____

   3. _____

   4. _____

Now write about something that might happen to you in the future where taking one step at a time might help you out: _____

_____

_____

Help yourself ahead of time by:

1) Identifying all the things that you will need to do: _____

_____

2) Putting them in order of importance:

   1. _____

   2. _____

   3. _____

   4. _____

CONGRATULATIONS! You have learned about how to take things one step at a time, and you have shown that you know how to use this Coping Skill. This is a way of taking care of yourself on the inside. **GREAT JOB!**

COPING SKILL 7:

BE KIND TO YOURSELF

Dealing with problems can be hard work. When you are working hard to take care of yourself, it is important to be kind to yourself; that can make the job a little easier.

Objective: To help children start thinking about what kind behavior entails.

Think about what it means to be kind. How do you act toward someone when you are treating him kindly? Write some of your ideas here:

_____

_____

_____

_____

Kindness can be shown in the way we talk, the words we use, the tone of our voice, and how we act. These are some specific ways of showing kindness:

   1) Stop what you're doing and pay attention.

   2) Use patience.

   3) Use gentle words.

These are things that we can do for others and also for ourselves. Paying attention means that you care enough about someone to spend time to listen to them. Using patience means that you try to relax and don't get mad quickly. Using gentle words can help someone feel better when she is having a problem.

Think about the difference between gentle words and harsh words. Can you think of some examples of each? Write them below:

Objective: To teach the difference between gentle and harsh words.

Gentle Words

Harsh Words

_____   _____

_____   _____

_____   _____

Stopping what you are doing and paying attention to yourself, using patience, and using gentle words are part of treating yourself with kindness. Treating yourself with kindness is a Coping Skill. It is a way of taking care of yourself when you have a problem. It is a way of taking care of yourself on the inside.

On the next pages, you will find a number of stories about kids who need to treat themselves with kindness. You can help them by: 1) Reminding them to pay attention to themselves; 2) Suggesting ways that they can use patience; and 3) Suggesting the words to use when they talk to themselves.

After you finish these stories, you will be asked to think about your own experiences with treating yourself kindly. As you answer the questions, you can use what you know about paying attention to yourself, using patience, and using gentle words to treat yourself kindly.

BE KIND TO YOURSELF

Objective: To give children hands-on experience in learning how to be self-nurturing through the use of patience and kind words; and a chance to apply that knowledge to their own lives.

Greg was the last one up to bat at his Little League softball practice. It was only his first season playing ball, and although he did pretty well in the outfield, he wasn't getting the hang of batting yet. Everyone was watching him and cheering for him. He swung at the pitch twice and missed. He swung at the third pitch and missed again. Greg felt terrible. He wondered how he could have missed every time. He figured he was the worst softball player in the world. He hung his head and walked off the field.

Help Greg by:

1) Reminding him to stop and pay attention to himself: _____

2) Suggesting a way for him to use patience: _____

_____

3) Suggesting kind words to use when he talks to himself: _____

_____

Maria had teeth that had grown in the wrong way. They were causing her problems, and the dentist had said it was important for her to get braces. She didn't want to wear braces because she thought they looked so dumb. There were some kinds of braces that didn't show in your mouth, but those were too expensive for her parents to afford. On the day she got her braces, Maria sat in her room looking at herself in the mirror. She looked at all the metal in her mouth. She thought she looked absolutely horrendous. She told herself she was the ugliest girl in school.

Help Maria by:

1) Reminding her to stop and pay attention to herself: _____

2) Suggesting a way for her to use patience: _____

_____

3) Suggesting kind words to use when she talks to herself:_____

_____

Aimee's class was starting a new chapter in their math books. They had been working with fractions for three days, and Aimee was having a hard time understanding how to work the problems. Her teacher had taken some extra time with her after school one day, but Aimee just felt more confused. She had turned in her homework and had gotten eight out of ten problems wrong. Aimee felt so stupid. Everybody else seemed to understand it; why couldn't she? She thought she must be the dumbest kid in school.

Help Aimee by:

1) Reminding her to stop and pay attention to herself: _____

2) Suggesting a way for her to use patience: _____

_____

3) Suggesting kind words to use when she talks to herself: _____

_____

BE KIND TO YOURSELF

Charlie was hoping to make some new friends when he started Boy Scouts. The first troop meeting he went to was one where the boys were finishing a woodworking project they had started the week before. Charlie tried to start conversations with the other boys, but they didn't seem to have much time for him; they were busy with their projects. He left the scout meeting feeling rejected. It seemed like no one wanted to be his friend. He felt lonely and out of place. He wondered why no one liked him. He wondered what was wrong with him.

Help Charlie by:

1) Reminding him to stop and pay attention to himself: _____

2) Suggesting a way for him to use patience: _____

_____

3) Suggesting kind words to use when he talks to himself: _____

_____

Merrilyn was learning to sew in her Home Economics class. She wanted to make her dad a chef's apron for his birthday, and she had found a pattern in the right size. But Merrilyn was having trouble with the sewing machine. She didn't seem to be able to adjust her speed, and almost every time she tried to sew a seam, the machine went too fast and she lost control. The needle would go off in the wrong direction, and she'd end up having to tear out all the stitches. Merrilyn was very discouraged. She thought she would never learn to sew. She told herself she was a failure, and her dad would probably hate his present.

Help Merrilyn by:

1) Reminding her to stop and pay attention to herself: _____

2) Suggesting a way for her to use patience: _____

_____

3) Suggesting kind words to use when she talks to herself: _____

_____

Tom had been meeting with a counselor at school because he had a hard time controlling his temper. He had been getting in fights with other students, and one time he had shouted at a teacher. Tom really wanted to stop fighting, but it felt like once he was irritated, his anger got worse fast; and then he couldn't control it. His dad was the same way and had been arrested once for starting a fight. Tom was trying to relax more and ignore some things other kids did that bothered him, but yesterday he blew up again and was sent to detention. Tom felt awful. He figured he must be just like his dad. He felt like he was cursed with this bad temper, and it would never go away. He felt like he was a very bad person.

Help Tom by:

1) Reminding him to stop and pay attention to himself: _____

2) Suggesting a way for him to use patience: _____

_____

3) Suggesting kind words to use when he talks to himself: _____

_____

Kara had gotten a pair of roller blades for her birthday, and she wanted to skate around the neighborhood with her friends; but she was having a hard time balancing. The other kids had roller blades for awhile already, and they went a lot faster than Kara and could do turns and stunts. Kara fell a lot and couldn't even stop by herself without skating onto the lawn. She was embarrassed and mad at herself. She told herself she was a total klutz and couldn't do anything right.

Help Kara by:

1) Reminding her to stop and pay attention to herself: _____

2) Suggesting a way for her to use patience: _____

_____

3) Suggesting kind words to use when she talks to herself: _____

_____

Chris's sister was two years older than him. Everywhere he went, people compared him to her. Especially in school. Chris's sister got very good grades in every class. Chris got average grades in every class. The teachers always asked him why his grades weren't as good as his sister's. He always tried his hardest, and he always passed; but he felt he was never good enough because he was never as good as his sister. Chris felt pretty dumb. He knew that no matter how hard he tried, he would never be as smart as his sister. He started to give up on his school work and didn't even try anymore. He figured he was just stupid, so why should he even try?

Help Chris by:

1) Reminding him to stop and pay attention to himself: _____

2) Suggesting a way for him to use patience: _____

_____

3) Suggesting kind words to use when he talks to himself: _____

_____

Write about something that happened to you recently where you would have benefitted by treating yourself kindly: _____

_____

_____

Help yourself by:

1) Reminding yourself to stop and pay attention to yourself: _____

2) Suggesting a way that you could have used patience: _____

_____

3) Suggesting kind words you could have used when you talked to yourself:

_____

_____

Now write about something that might happen to you in the future where treating your self kindly might help you out: _____

_____

_____

Help yourself by:

1) Reminding yourself to stop and pay attention to yourself: _____

2) Suggesting a way that you could use patience: _____

_____

3) Suggesting kind words to use when you talk to yourself: _____

_____

CONGRATULATIONS! You have learned about how to treat yourself kindly, and you have shown that you know how to use this Coping Skill. This is a way of taking care of yourself on the inside. **WAY TO GO!**

COPING SKILL 8:

PLAN AHEAD

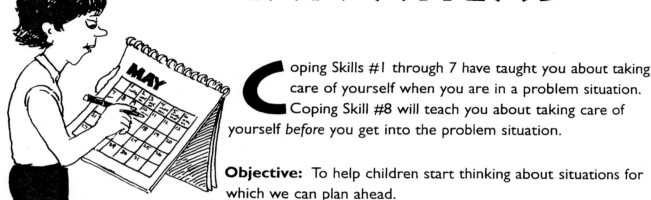

Coping Skills #1 through 7 have taught you about taking care of yourself when you are in a problem situation. Coping Skill #8 will teach you about taking care of yourself *before* you get into the problem situation.

Objective: To help children start thinking about situations for which we can plan ahead.

Sometimes we know about things before they happen, like knowing that you have to go to school every morning. Sometimes we don't know about things until they happen, like when you fall off of your bike. Can you think of some other things that you know about before they happen? Write them here: _____

_____

_____

Objective: To help children understand the difference between situations we can plan ahead for and those we can't.

What are some things you don't know about until they happen? Write them here:

_____

_____

_____

When we know about things ahead of time, we can prepare for them, or plan ahead. This is a way of taking care of ourselves. Just like Coping Skill #6 (Taking Things One Step at a Time), Coping Skill #8, Planning Ahead, is a way to keep ourselves from feeling overwhelmed. When we plan something ahead of time, we feel more prepared to handle it.

Objective: To scale down the exercise into workable parts.

Pick one thing from your list that you know about before it happens. Write it again here:

_____

_____

_____

Objective: To give children practice in thinking about what it means to plan ahead.

Now think about what you can plan to do ahead of time to prepare for this. Write your answer here:

_____

_____

_____

Planning ahead can assure that we will:

1) Have enough time. 2) Have enough energy. 3) Have the tools to accomplish our task.

Planning ahead can help to keep you from becoming overwhelmed. This is a Coping Skill. It is a way of taking care of yourself when you have a problem. It is a way to take care of yourself on the inside.

On the next pages, you will find a number of stories about kids who need to plan ahead. You can help them by: 1) Suggesting things they can do to be sure they will have enough time and energy; and 2) Suggesting how they can be sure to have the tools they will need to accomplish their task.

After you finish these stories, you will be asked to think about your own experiences with planning ahead. As you answer the questions, you can use what you know about making sure you have enough time and energy and the tools you will need to help yourself.

Objective: To give children hands-on experience in preventing problems by planning ahead; and a chance to apply that knowledge to their own lives.

On Thursday, Derek's teacher announced that there would be a big social studies test the following Monday. She reminded each student to study extra hard over the weekend and to be sure to read the next chapter in the book. Derek didn't know how he was going to study over the weekend, because he was supposed to go camping with his dad early Saturday morning, and they weren't coming home until late Sunday night.

Help Derek by:

1) Suggesting what he can do to be sure he has enough time and energy:

_____

_____

2) Suggesting how he can make sure he has the tools he needs: _____

_____

_____

Sherrie wants to make Valentines for all of her friends this year. She's not sure if she should mail them or just hand them out at school. She has to get markers and paper, and she's thinking about lace, or maybe stickers. She doesn't know if she has enough envelopes. She's a little worried, because last year she tried to make Valentines and only got two done in time.

Help Sherrie by:

1) Suggesting what she can do to be sure she has enough time and energy:

_____

_____

2) Suggesting how she can make sure she has the tools she needs: _____

_____

Ginny wants to give her friend, Sara, a surprise birthday party. Ginny's mom said she could have the party in their basement, but Ginny has to do all the planning and cleaning up. Sara's birthday is one month away. Ginny has to invite the guests, decorate the house, bake a cake, plan games, and buy a present for Sara. She wants all of Sara's friends to come, and she doesn't want Sara to find out.

Help Ginny by:

1) Suggesting what she can do to be sure she has enough time and energy:

_____

_____

2) Suggesting how she can make sure she has the tools she needs: _____

_____

_____

Mark has trouble remembering to do his homework. He always plans to do it, but sometimes he forgets his books at school; or when he does bring them home, he drops them in the hall and then forgets them. He gets something to eat and turns on the TV. It feels good to relax after a long day at school. Sometimes his friends come over, or he goes to one of their houses. Mark's mom comes home and makes dinner, and Mark helps her clean up the kitchen and get his younger sister to bed. Then he lies down in his room and listens to his stereo for awhile. At 9 o'clock, Mark's mom asks him if his homework is done. Mark says that he meant to do it, but now he's too tired; and it's too late anyway. He usually gets marked down a grade for not turning in his work on time.

Help Mark by:

1) Suggesting what he can do to make sure he has enough time and energy:

_____

_____

2) Suggesting how he can make sure he has the tools he needs: _____

_____

_____

Lianne is on the swim team at the YMCA. There is going to be an all-day swim meet next Saturday. Lianne will have to compete in four different events. The meet starts at 8 a.m. and won't be over until 6 p.m. The swim coach told all the swimmers to be sure they're in good shape for the meet. Lianne had originally planned to go to a slumber party on Friday night. She knows if she goes to the party she may stay up all night.

Help Lianne by:

1) Suggesting what she can do to make sure she has enough time and energy:

_____

2) Suggesting how she can make sure she has the tools she needs: _____

_____

orey's favorite band is coming to town, and he wants to see them in concert. His mom said she'll drive Corey and his friends, but he has to pay for the ticket himself. Corey usually earns money by mowing lawns, but the lawn mower is broken. He has $7 saved in his wallet, but he needs $20 more. There are two weeks left until the concert. His brother said he would lend Corey the money if he has enough, but he won't know until the day before the concert.

Help Corey by:

1) Suggesting what he can do to make sure he has enough time and energy:

_____

_____

2) Suggesting how he can make sure he has the tools he needs: _____

_____

_____

Jack comes from a family of nine. He has five brothers and three sisters. Jack's mom works full time, so she needs a lot of help around the house. Jack's job is to do laundry, but he can never find the time to do it all; and when he does start, he usually runs out of detergent before all the clothes are done. Jack has a paper route that he does every evening. On weekends, he goes to his dad's house. On Tuesdays and Thursdays, he stays after school for extra help in reading. There never seems to be enough clean clothes.

Help Jack by:

1) Suggesting what he can do to make sure he has enough time and energy:

_____

_____

2) Suggesting how he can make sure he has the tools he needs: _____

_____

_____

Write about something that happened to you recently where you would have benefitted from planning ahead: _____

_____

_____

Help yourself by:

1) Suggesting what you could have done to make sure you had enough time and energy:

_____

_____

2) Suggesting how you could have made sure you had the tools you needed:

_____

_____

Now, write about something that might happen to you in the future where planning ahead will help you out: _____

_____

_____

Help yourself by:

1) Suggesting what you can do ahead of time to make sure you have enough time and energy:

_____

_____

2) Suggesting how you can make sure that you will have the tools you need:

_____

_____

CONGRATULATIONS! You have learned about how to plan ahead, and you have shown that you know how to use this Coping Skill. This is a way of taking care of yourself on the inside.
EXCELLENT WORK!

COPING SKILL 9:

ASK FOR HELP

The last Coping Skill that you will learn about has to do with recognizing when a problem situation is too big for you to take care of completely by yourself. When that happens, it's time for Coping Skill #9: Ask For Help.

No matter how good we become at handling things by ourselves, there will always be times when we need to ask someone else to help us. Sometimes people think they should be able to do everything by themselves, or that asking for help means that they've failed, or that they're not as strong or as smart as they should be.

The truth is, even the strongest and smartest people can't do everything by themselves. Earlier in this book, we learned that because we are all human beings, no one is perfect (Coping Skill #4: Accept Imperfection). In the same way, we all need help from others at one time or another.

Objective: To help children apply set forth ideas to their own lives.

Can you think of something you did recently where you needed to ask for help? Write it here:

_____

_____

_____

_____

Objective: To help children understand that even parents need to ask for help sometimes.

Can you think of something your mom or dad did recently where they asked for help? Write it here:

_____

_____

_____

Objective: To help children understand that all people need to ask for help at some time; this is normal, and not a sign of weakness.

Can you think of something your teacher did recently where she or he asked for help? Write it here:

_____

_____

Asking for help doesn't mean that you have failed, or even that you aren't trying your hardest. When you have done all you can by yourself, and can't seem to get any further, asking for help is smart. This is a Coping Skill. It is a way of taking care of yourself when you have a problem. It is a way of taking care of yourself on the inside.

On the next pages, you will find a number of stories about kids who can't solve their problems all by themselves.

You can help them by: 1) Pointing out the effort they have already made; and 2) Suggesting how they could ask for help.

After you finish these stories, you will be asked to think about your own experiences with asking for help. As you answer the questions, you can use what you know about recognizing when you have done all you can do by yourself and how you can ask for help.

ASK FOR HELP

Objective: To give children hands-on experience in learning that everyone needs help from others at some time, and that it is appropriate and important to seek this help when we cannot cope with a problem by ourselves; and a chance to apply that knowledge to their own lives.

Stacey is home alone after school. The phone rings, but when she answers it, no one is there; so she hangs up. A few minutes later, the phone rings again, and this time she only hears someone breathing. Stacey figures it is a prank call and slams the receiver down hard like her mom told her to do. In a little while, the phone rings again. She tries to ignore it, but it keeps ringing and ringing, so finally she picks it up. This time a voice says, "I know you're home alone." Stacey hangs up the phone quickly. She wants to act grown up and take care of herself, but she feels scared.

Help Stacey by:

1) Pointing out the effort she's already made: _____

_____

2) Suggesting how she could ask for help: _____

_____

Keenan has been feeling sad a lot lately. His Uncle Carl, to whom he was very close, was killed in a car accident last month. Uncle Carl didn't have any kids of his own, so he liked to spend a lot of time with Keenan. He took him to movies, and go-carting, and fishing at the river in the summertime. Keenan can't seem to stop thinking about Uncle Carl. His mom said it was normal for him to be sad and that he would get over it eventually. But Keenan only seems to feel worse each day. Some days he hasn't been going to school; he just lies in his bed all day. On the days he does go to school, he can't seem to concentrate. He hasn't done any homework in over a week.

Help Keenan by:

1) Pointing out the effort he's already made: _____

_____

2) Suggesting how he could ask for help: _____

_____

olleen is getting very frustrated with her schoolwork. She has always been a slow reader, but she has been able to keep up with the class by working extra hard. Lately, though, each subject has involved more reading assignments, and she never seems to finish one before the next one is assigned. She is also feeling confused because, even when she does do the reading, she doesn't always understand what she has read. Colleen has been staying up late trying to catch up, but then she has trouble staying awake in school the next day. She is so tired of trying, she's ready to give up.

Help Colleen by:

1) Pointing out the effort she's already made: _____

_____

2) Suggesting how she could ask for help: _____

_____

_____

For the last three days, when Rob has left school, four boys have followed him and threatened to beat him up if he didn't do what they asked. One day they made him give them all his money; one day they ripped up his homework; the third day they took his baseball cap and cut it up with a knife. Rob has tried ignoring them, running away from them, and leaving the school by different doors, but the boys always find him. Rob doesn't want anyone to think he's chicken, but he's afraid of what the boys might do next. He knows they are part of a gang from another school.

Help Rob by:

1) Pointing out the effort he's already made: _____

_____

2) Suggesting how he could ask for help: _____

_____

_____

Andrea has been getting headaches lately. She wakes up feeling OK in the morning, but by lunchtime her head is feeling tense; and usually by the end of the school day, it is aching badly. She knows she's not supposed to take pills without asking her mother, but one day she took some children's aspirin because it hurt so much. The headache went away but came back again the next day. Andrea also noticed that it is hard for her to see the blackboard from her seat in the back of the classroom, and her eyes tend to get blurry when she reads a lot. She tries closing her eyes to rest them, but that doesn't seem to help.

Help Andrea by:

1) Pointing out the effort she's already made: _____

_____

2) Suggesting how she could ask for help: _____

_____

_____

Denise is baking cookies for the bake sale at school. She wants to make them all by herself without any help from her mom. She gets out the cookbook and all of the ingredients. She mixes everything together the way the recipe says. She puts the cookie dough onto cookie sheets. But then she gets stuck. The cookbook says to preheat the oven, and Denise isn't sure how to do that. There are no knobs on the stove labeled "preheat." When she turns one knob, flames come out of the gas burner. She turns it off again quickly but is stuck as to what to do next.

Help Denise by:

1) Pointing out the effort she's already made: _____

_____

2) Suggesting how she could ask for help: _____

_____

Jared is taking a test at school. The teacher has said there should be no talking during the test, and anyone caught cheating will get an immediate "F." But when Jared looks at the second page of his test, he discovers that the copy machine has blurred all the words in the directions. He can't read what he is supposed to do on the second page. He raises his hand, but the teacher has left the room for a few minutes. Jared could ask his neighbor what the directions on his clear paper say. Or, if he stretched his neck far enough, he could see the paper on the student's desk in front of him. He waits for awhile, but the teacher doesn't return.

Help Jared by:

1) Pointing out the effort he's already made: _____

_____

2) Suggesting how he could ask for help: _____

_____

Brian has learned enough about drugs at school to know that they are dangerous. He has better things to with his life than get sick or die from taking drugs. One day he sees two kids behind the school smoking something that smells awful. They tell him it is marijuana and ask him to try it. Brian refuses and goes out to the field to play ball with his friends. Later, Brian sees the same boys showing the marijuana to some little kids. One of the kids is his little brother, who tells Brian that those boys have tried several times to get him to try it. Brian is worried; he doesn't want anything bad to happen to his brother or the other little kids.

Help Brian by:

1) Pointing out the effort he's already made: _____

_____

2) Suggesting how he could ask for help: _____

_____

_____

ASK FOR HELP

Jenny's cousin, Brad, gives her the creeps. He is a lot older than her, and he looks at her in funny ways. Sometimes he bumps into her or brushes against her for no reason at all. One day, when Brad and his family come to visit, Jenny's mom sends Brad and Jenny to the store for some ice cream. On the way home, Brad grabs Jenny and tries to touch her under her clothes. Jenny tells him to stop and pushes him away, but Brad just gets mad. He says if she tells anyone what happened, he'll get her in big trouble.

Help Jenny by:

1) Pointing out the effort she's already made: _____

_____

2) Suggesting how she could ask for help: _____

_____

Write about something that happened to you recently where you could have asked for help to make things better: _____

_____

Help yourself by:

1) Pointing out the effort you made by yourself: _____

_____

2) Suggesting how you could have asked for help: _____

_____

Now, write about something that might happen to you in the future where asking for help could make things better: _____

_____

_____

Help yourself ahead of time by:

1) Pointing out the effort you could make by yourself first: _____

_____

2) Suggesting how you could ask for help: _____

_____

CONGRATULATIONS! You have learned about how to ask for help, and you have shown that you know how to use this Coping Skill. This is a way of taking care of yourself on the inside. **GOOD EFFORT!**

COPING SKILLS REVIEW

Objective: To review the skills learned in this book.

You learned about nine different coping skills in this book. Can you remember them all? Write them below:

1. _____

2. _____

3. _____

4. _____

5. _____

6. _____

7. _____

8. _____

9. _____

On the next pages, you will find a number of stories about kids who are in problem situations. After you read the stories, you can help each child by: 1) Identifying which coping skills they could use to help themselves; and 2) Explaining specifically what each child could do to put that skill into action.

After you finish these stories, you will find space to write a story about yourself using the coping skills in a real-life problem situation.

Objective: To help children integrate and reinforce their knowledge of all 9 coping skills, and to understand how the skills can work together in different situations.

Dane is lying in his room listening to his CD player. He rereads the list of chores his stepfather has given him, and then he rips it up into little pieces and throws them onto the floor. He pounds his fists into his mattress. He doesn't want to do anything on that list—in fact, he doesn't want to do anything at all. Ever since his mom married his stepfather, Dane's life has been miserable. He hates having his stepfather living in his house. He wants his real dad to be here; he misses his dad so much. When his parents divorced, his dad moved out of the state, so Dane only gets to see him during school vacations. He hates it that his dad is so far away. He hates taking orders from his stepfather. He feels miserable in school, and he feels miserable at home. He doesn't even have much fun with his friends anymore.

Help Dane by:

1) Identifying which coping skills he could use to help himself:

_____

_____

2) Explaining specifically what he needs to do to put each skill into action:

_____

_____

Nicole feels like she's going crazy. Her little sister, Michelle, will not stop crying. She won't sit still for more than a few minutes, and she isn't even any fun to play with. Nicole had been a little excited when her mom was pregnant. It seemed like it might be fun to have a new baby in the house. But it didn't turn out anything like Nicole had hoped. Michelle has Attention Deficit Disorder, which means it is very hard for her to play quietly or to concentrate on one thing for more than a few minutes at a time. Now all Nicole's parents seem to do is pay attention to Michelle. They don't seem to have any time for Nicole anymore. They are always telling her how Michelle takes up so much of their energy, so Nicole is supposed to be on her best behavior all the time. Nicole is so sick of Michelle and her problem. Sometimes she wishes her little sister had never been born.

Help Nicole by:

1) Identifying which coping skills she could use to help herself:

_____

_____

2) Explaining specifically what she needs to do to put each skill into action:

_____

_____

Gretta tried to get her eyes to open, but she kept falling back to sleep. She was so tired. She couldn't believe it was morning already. She wished she didn't have to go to school today; she wished she could just roll over and go back to sleep. But today there was a science test, and today she had to give her oral report in social studies. And, she still hadn't finished her book report for English. She had planned to get up early and do it before school this morning, but she had stayed up late last night watching a movie on TV. She hadn't turned off the light until 3 a.m. Gretta had a one-hour study hall for her first class of the day. Maybe she could go back to sleep and go to school late. Maybe she should tell her mom she was sick. She felt scared when she thought of the day ahead. She didn't know how she was going to get through it.

Help Gretta by:

1) Identifying which coping skills she could use to help herself:

_____

_____

2) Explaining specifically what she needs to do to put each skill into action:

_____

_____

COPING SKILLS REVIEW

G rant was dreading the next day. It would be the second day at his new school. The first day had been awful. Grant was the only black student in his class. There were a few other black kids in the school, but he only saw them passing in the halls. Grant's old school had had an even mix of black and white and Hispanic kids. There, he had many friends. In this school, he felt out of place. He had tried talking to some boys in the cafeteria, and they had been nice; but he still felt uncomfortable. It seemed that all the other kids knew each other already. Grant felt very alone and a little scared. At his old school, he had been on the basketball team, but he didn't know if he wanted to try out at this school. He just wished he could go back to his old school and his old friends where he felt comfortable and at home.

Help Grant by:

1) Identifying which coping skills he could use to help himself:

_____

_____

2) Explaining specifically what he needs to do to put each skill into action:

_____

_____

Think about a problem situation that you have been dealing with lately. Write about

what it is like:

_____

_____

Now, help yourself by:

1) Identifying which coping skills you could use to help yourself:

_____

_____

2) Explaining specifically what you need to do to put each skill into action:

_____

_____

_____

CONGRATULATIONS! You've learned to take care of yourself on the "inside"—to deal with your problems by expressing your thoughts and feelings. You've mastered the coping skills, and here's your award!

Objective: To reward children for their efforts, raise self-esteem.

CONGRATULATIONS!

_____
Name

You have learned to take care of yourself on the inside. You can deal with your problems by expressing your thoughts and feelings. You've mastered the nine Coping Skills!

_____
Date